blue heron

The Mountain West Poetry Series
Stephanie G'Schwind & Donald Revell, series editors

We Are Starved, by Joshua Kryah
The City She Was, by Carmen Giménez Smith
Upper Level Disturbances, by Kevin Goodan
The Two Standards, by Heather Winterer
Blue Heron, by Elizabeth Robinson

blue heron elizabeth robinson

poems

The Center for Literary Publishing
Colorado State University

For information about permission to reproduce
selections from this book, write to
Permissions, Center for Literary Publishing,
9105 Campus Delivery, Department of English,
Colorado State University,
Fort Collins, Colorado 80523-9105.

Printed in the United States of America.

Library of Congress Cataloging-in-Publication Data

Robinson, Elizabeth, 1961-
[Poems. Selections]
Blue heron : poems / Elizabeth Robinson.
        pages ; cm. -- (The mountain west poetry series)
ISBN 978-1-885635-29-7 (pbk. : alk. paper) --
ISBN 978-1-885635-30-3 (electronic)
I. Title.

PS3568.O2883A6 2013
811'.54--dc23

2013017275

The paper used in this book meets the minimum requirements of the
American National Standard for Information Sciences-Permanence of
Paper for Printed Library Materials, ANSI z39.48-1984.

1 2 3 4 5   17 16 15 14 13

This book is for Sasquatch, who does exist.

contents

lynx rufus

The forefeet predict the hind

as though

a paw print were a target.

Feet responding to their own recent absence: that is,

a body lands where it's been. Immediately.

                                        Hears a suspicion.

A body holding its own dusk.

That is what a predator is, mostly

unseen, by which is meant: it may abound. Commonly

hungry.

The body knows its dusk is food because the half-light is prey

in a world made solely of meat. It knows

only meat.

Gravity, too, is meat, and so the hind feet pounce on the forefeet

though they are already gone.

The sound of air is a scent,

a shape made of its own structure.

Ear tuft, face ruff, stub tail.

Furred casing on the act

of the chase, piss-warning, fast.

Taut loitering.

The horizon is sure only insofar as

it hides itself.

The ground beneath the body is made of flesh,

or it is useless.

Pallor at lips and chin.

Soundless mouth; mating

mouth, solitary

appetite.

The claws retract to their rocky ledge, feral with thickets,

transient stench of

range.   Makes passage

on the hips of the undisclosed creature.

cherimoya

The tongue conformed itself

around this large, glossy darkness,

a groove cut from its own kernel, whose tartness cut

the overwhelming sweetness of the tongue congealing

around the seed.

The very notion of sweetness, what is sweetness, how does the flesh

cloy to its core, the buttery white flesh

of the tongue.

It had no

meaning in itself, only that it gathered

and recorded the seeds to its milky, furred breast,

an embrace meant to

disclose that the tongue was ready and

redundant in its velvet pocket of flesh.

_____quarry

The ankle of the weather twists.

What had seemed,

ceased to seem.

Then, *away* didn't mean escape, it simply meant *nature*.

A safe, small promontory into the water.

                    Ankle, now weather,
                    predator, wing.

This-that-we-know

is a spoiled wing, bent feather.

Whereas weather

has a body all its own.

Were I to go away,

I would, by

weight of saying,

say less.

Trauma

drowned by its own skirts.

Trauma

is quaint, a dream in one dialect,

food in the next

                                                              that weighs the air away.

was that, a wing in

practical, quaint flight.

The skirt on practicality
now bears down on one as hunger.

The wing walks slowly, safe,

          not here.

                           Smaller

               promontory into a body of water.

The skirt on the landform is practical, sensible, a form

of water, once a form of *gone*

but no longer such a garment.

Was walking a form of weather, a form

of following, falling from the form

as it twists?

The weather was mispronounced, was an inversion

of following, a promontory turned.

It was not a twist. Trauma:

neither safe nor unsafe. The burden

of the skirt dragging in water. Quarry
susceptible to the cloak of its hunter.

Dead mass of walking—no—not that, but

      dialect of

walking

as nature, always hunger, away.

What was once ease

of swimming, flying.
Adjust

famine as

meaning for its end. Weight

durably, hungrily undresses. The landmass

I was did not dissolve, just

turned away

from the wing's broken load.

It was cold.

Sodden, or water repellent.

I was the ankle.

Spiral.

I was wing after all, mispromontory, predator.

the hinge trees

Here is where you were.

They were unknown hinges. And

you thought

you could speak in them. Absurd that a dead tree

could speak in poetics. Dead trees.

So you needed a human to come and say the words for you. In increments,

the way a child stumbles through a script written in an adult's

hand. The way

the hinges were sockets, but possibly

not joints, possibly not articulated.

Your immediate physical presence is always spoken from memory.

I mean: vertically.

I mean that a thing who seems continuous is made up of two parts.

A perimeter around the invisible:

I didn't mean any such denigrating term as *thing*.

I meant person.

A person who seems continuous is made up of two things.

From there, you arc upward, lost.

The perimeter around the invisible is a person.

You said, as a chorus, "What do you know about persons?"

"What," I asked, "do you know about bareness?"

"What is illegible writing?"

It was in the nature of the question to seem an accusation, to congregate as a series of spines, whiter and whiter as they arced to the sky, to seem to be writing back a breeze when the breeze was so invisible as not to move.

Who made that question?

An immobile breeze is more or less like a root: present but not manifest.

Is our argument done? Did we put together a poetics

that softened your disappointment with words?

If we plant

one live sapling for each dead hinge tree, will

you permit the saplings to become ghosts to your deadness?

Yes. You will permit the saplings to become persons.

There is where you were, and now, here.

Overhead.

Poetics measures the difference between a socket and a hinge.

The degree to which the breeze potentially begins to move.

I did not think you were inanimate. That is what I clarify. I thought
you were anchored, until you followed me back. The relation of dead trees
to a breeze.

Faltering, I clarify you.

blue heron

i.

The heron dies.

The food sent to his stomach

abets him no more.

His urine turns black.

But his face remains blue; his face

and its grizzled beard

have agreed to be turned thus

by blue hands

to the standard of the sky.

Those whose flight is stolen from them

still have this. So did his daughter

witness, collecting the glaze on the

discarded food, the rupture

of his heart, where she folded

a rib cage or otherwise

made a bed for the body

he could settle into. This shoulder,

this wing, this odious

resignation.

ii.

An angry form

of levitation,
the ugly bird

defines flight,
gnawing with its blue beak, with

its little flaring
nostril alighting on
blue air.

Little and mean,
this downwardness
the man-bird belches out,

dies passively,
appears dead,

gets up again.

Flipped: up
in the wet air.

Between.

We loft on hybrid air.

     What makes us

     (kindred)

     that we can so exhaust ourselves?

     Can we pinpoint

     why a creature is a creature?

Because, at final leave-taking,

we are intermediary to each other?

     Claw and quill and horrific cliff.

     Froth of reason, hardening. The tremor of the filial, striving

to hover midway, to be final.

Little man, do you

eat blue feathers? Rigid,

do you

tarry here, guard

of trespass?
Do I

repeat myself

as I eat

myself, foreordained:

the furious man

borne

where air burns

feather, the falling

trespass, its burnt

metabolism. Sugar-

wing. Furious

saccharine froth ignited

in the air. Quills

pierce its engorged

airborne cheek.

What

bestows itself from

the almost-invisible

and its stain. What claw

or hand.

Whoever it was

that saw no cause

in the bird that he

be a bird, whoever

it was that would

leave in disrepair—

these ashes, this hand,

or otherwise the pure

idea of color, the cliff

that curls and crumbles

into whom: dust purer

than tint.

Whose eye peered through the stranded
shore

and the creature large and blue
saw, and forced

eye back.

Stealthy, the creature circled
itself, circled

itself in vine and water,

its blue and gold throat.

Radiant as
iris around pupil,

slippery enclosure
the grove of

sight makes. Were

vision purely hostile

the eye blurs, swallows,

       and forces back the stream,

the blue, covert green.

Daughter

was the word

for the gaze. The one who looked hard

against the passive world. The body on its back

looks up at the sky, hard. Daughter of man or bird

is daughter of time, of confusion. The word made its own

memorial, as the eye blinks. The shadow overhead, over,

over again.

Each species walks backward
from waterline
to dry path.

It happens
that they may bump
into each other.

      The burdens of those on earth
are based on
their level of grief when their

shoulders collide.

Each species can be forced,
by the pressure of the gaze that observes them,
to look alike.

      (The mouth held just so
        as the body strides
        backward.)

The air, at the site of the
collision, develops an opaline
tinge:

      a judgment
      of difference that proximity
      cannot fix.

Whose is the rage

and therefore rage as proof

that this is, none of it, a dream,

even as it shimmers—

this disavowal of dreams, this

wanderer thrashing through the

path and startling the creature,

as proof that despair is

true, is justifiable, that the breach

is its own fact even when it releases, briefly

clinging from one to the other like

a fume in the atmosphere.

Ungainly bird,

the anguished—

the man—refutes the table where he rests,

and there he defies

his winged hands set atop it.

      Abomination, he spits:

      lagoon, blue-skinned bird, dreadful

      size.

Rescind the bird's tongue and

it will go away to upbraid

song. Give it back to the man,

the beak, the distress deaf to

all interruption before a face, his avian face.

        Sodden, on this table

      he resides, and so subsides:

        boggled, bobbing,

      captured by its whiplashed dimension.

xi.

We are forced to fly, yet we

are not kin, or were we—

       soft, infectious rhythm

       passing on air?

Strange pleasure, the gift of gliding above ground

where the daughter sees him, and he, easily,

above the dead or singular.

Refusal to see the shock

of yellow, the claw treading the ground

       surreptitiously alive. Grim

in its discrimination between

the lost and a version

       of life, skimming, sparse, above its own weight.

xii.

In this language, we have no interest in your bird-like attributes.

What fascinates is the ease with which

you are able to drift between species.

Were you

to eat a leaf

from the local bush,

its branch

becomes a switch

so that we are able

to beat you.

Fast you transform

while the whip of the air

sings on its own wing.

I carry a small and furious man
in the pouch of my cheek.

Night cheek, blue cheek, not
man, not heron.

      I permit the ocean to fling itself at
      his back
      to frighten him.

Or I disturb my own wing

to foster him.

The quills of feathers

grow under my tongue
before I tear them out

for my wing. This he knows
where knowledge is liable

to swallow itself.

The crest of his cloud-immersed
head signals where I am to find him,

whereas the pouch of my beak
says no less.

Say you came back to a site

where you saw

what you saw—

      What on return you saw

        is that you could see it no more.

The question not meant to be airborne

nonetheless flew

away awkward

on its internal air.

I could not stop for the creature, for

the wild animal,

for emptying sand from my shoes,
for swallowing again my own distress
and again

my distress swallowing, it

awaiting.

       Startle. The seawater rush of blood

in my throat and

this I suck onto my tongue
and force back down my throat.

The least tangible presence
was the one I spat out most bluntly.

Thus he waited for me.

His slender blue throat, his unwillingness, his gray face.

Blunt body of human vomiting itself through the path,

feral, unruly, disquieted.

He was his own demise I sipped, and
loss gagging itself, its narrow, elegant throat

come upon, unattended, awaiting. Beak and lip,

and then he did not wait longer.

Daughter stumbles on the pavement,
seeing,

and the skin is rubbed off
the mystery:

the eye beholds
through the shrubs,

and what it beholds
            the shadow contains.

She clutches her leg and hand
to the hurt
in the bend of the body.

Her blood

has certitude

just as her eye
held in its socket

looks surely to the boundary of the shrubs.

        Aloft,

wounded, and

like the shrub, chafed

by sight, by the stumbling

seer.

Grass, the horizon that it implies. A world clean in the mouth.

Beneath that, the smear of the sky. Ongoing hunger.

Beneath that, the character who plays charades.

Lower and lower.

All you may not surmount.

Modesty is its own refusal,

fizzing. Representative

of the overhanging

sky.

The anniversary

of the word. What word

is it,

hollowed of all its

meaning, and so

the perfect carrier: the word

that failed gravity

tastes as bitter. Poison

was the word, and buoyant.

He is outside and all has been stolen from him

—even species, even pulse—

and his distress is now

complete. His long form softens the sketch

of his posture,

and he leans on the empty sill:

      the perturbed and the imperturbable, so familiar—

      if not the place, then the stride

      that moves toward it.

      Once his stride was long

      and now it is lurching.

Once a line could be drawn

straight through the uprightness of

      the gap. Eccentric nest.

    Now the picture is

scrawled by one who is left-handed,

whose hand blurs the lines it draws

all the way down.

xx.

Daughter is the eye

that measures a presence now gone.

The eye that moves as horizon and sees the horizon

jackknife into absence.

The eye sees the man,

the eye sees the magic bird keening silently,

and through binocular vision the two merge.

Daughter is the eye that sees death with its

blue water-repellent feathers. Then the crushed

smell of fennel where the two eyes gaze in concert,

disconcerted as blindness on the blunt path

as it opens onto vacancy.

Daughter has insisted, put my ashes:

here.

What is an ash but

the venom on presence.

What is given

but a riddle.

The waves break and they are foamy and they know

their discretion is dangerous. Riddle.

The ash, meaning absence, captures the spume and stings the eye.

xxii.

The story wants to do justice to its repetition.

The wing in its monotonous motion tires everything around it, except memory.

hibernaculum

A bone cannot tell a bone's story   nor a cave

a cave's

this trinket of life of

having lived   spinning

on the unsanctioned air

overcome with its whiteness

                              the cloud

arrived gray unless   its whiteness

is blind after which

                              no weather

sounds   resounds

                how   in this renunciation

the bone reveres itself   how

                                              trading

silence for color

dust of the bone

broken   white   underfoot

of what hollow tread

whose marrow infects   its inhabitants

of who   and then

how   the breathing

organs are caked
                                        the caves'

with their own habitation

and white core

a cave once was a cloud

        upon the bones   fading

collects like dew   lacework

of claws where the obscurity

clings   cloud upended

is a cavern   a cup   sleep's

closure

what is possible

is white   and what is sleep

covers this white

with   other whiteness   belling in

in the empty haze

of its finish   polish

               a cloud

has come   lodged

on its own residue   animate

dust on its own

addendum of

sleep on bafflement   blur   flimsy

on weather

overlayer of purpose

brought forth

to admire

pallor's rime

sifting marrow
                    here, our

lung   where air lost

to itself   quaver   is not

        dark   wan   color

echo   as a cloud and a bone

so   but oh   estranged

further   from the white cave   still

the breathing creature

loves its other   hovering

over its nostrils as another

weightlessness of meaning

the endless   breath   farther

                                        stilling

on monsters

It is not painful to be unseen. Sasquatch

crouches in the forest primeval, eucalyptus,

coded topiary.

It is not a disability to bear the disability

of being unseen.

He who likes to walk from one terrain to the next, that one
is a monster.

A keen sense of smell is better than all the articulable joints

of any given word. Fennel, wild

rosemary, rose hips.

We

steal plums, forage in the blackberry bramble.

Odor of prehistory.

Ache-odor of sea.

Clumsy opposable thumb of hand to mouth.

To be a monster, Yeti thinks,
is to know that life is not so long as she once thought it was.

And also: that time may move very slowly.

Slowly.

To be unseen and to fail to speak

is to use the plural pronoun "we" sparingly.

One monster turns south, lies on her left side, and so prepares to sleep.

One monster.

Time spews itself out in so many directions.

Didn't "monster" imply
narrative? There is no narrative, only the narrative that the monster was not
sure he saw.

The terrain grew achy and out of sorts with its unfinding.

Sasquatch sweats profusely, but not from illness. From exertion. From sunlight.

Yeti is woken up.

Scent and taste can stand in for one another, interchangeable
signatures of time.

A body wakes up inside its invisibility and is no less invisible.

She can smell the verb of another

monster. The stride of invisibility covering so much terrain.

If only.   Here,

take a look at the contingency

of the monstrous.

Sasquatch follows the skyline to look east and flat.

Yeti stands in the shade, studying the fine blue hair on her face, her thighs.

If here.

The pace of time has its own scent that could be tracked past any originary site to a meeting point.

Monster or beast: one who walks.

When a monster finally opens its mouth, it sings terribly off-key, but behind teeth and palate it can taste what it wants to say with faultless accuracy.

Its ancestors gave their young poison oak leaves to chew, so they would build tolerance to its poison,

sing inflamed tunes.

What, again, is a monster?

One who wears the disguise of tranquility,

who smells of seawater and bruise.

One who is accurate (and therefore disabled) in crisis.

We

who are so subject to category
refuse to be of interest, are not

interested in those who impute the mythic to the real.

Bay leaf

Oak, poison oak

Those whose contingency is wasted on honey will eat bees.

Manzanita

To be free of the burden of evidence.

A monster's disability is to be free, where

to be a suspicion is also to adopt suspicion.

To steal freely from one's own garden.

To have thus far evaded witness.

To watch one's self.

Like time: steep.

At the sharpest incline of the hill, a monster may turn around and walk backward

up.

Scree, talus, a dead squirrel whose carcass is filled with wasps.

Where a hand reaches, reaches into the cleft of itself, and a rock

shows time's deformation, ground into a mortar, a presence that

was former

eroded into the present.

That is, the bizarre gentleness of the monster,

our imperceptible monster,

asks that we

"leave

the roots on, let them

dangle."

As roots also quicken, bruise their plural pronouns, lose tune,

forsake terrain by moving through and on it.

acknowledgements

"Lynx Rufus" was published in *Poetic Inventory*.
("Large as a bird") and ("Little man, do you") were published in *Zoland Magazine*.
("The heron dies.") appeared on the Counterpath Press website.
Bombay Gin and *Longhouse* published the other sections of "Blue Heron."
"Cherimoya" appeared in *Eoagh* and "Quarry" was first published in *Set*.
"The Hinge Trees" was published in *Conjunctions Online*.
"Hiburnaculum" was published as part of the chapbook *Phrases/Fragments*.
"On Monsters" was first published as a Little Red Leaves, Textile Series Chapbook.
Many thanks to the editors who first printed this work.

My particular gratitude to Chana Bloch
for a generous and insightful reading of this manuscript.

I am grateful to the Lynden Sculpture Garden and Woodland Pattern
in Milwaukee, Wisconsin, and the Djerassi Resident Artists' Program in Woodside,
California, for residencies that were instrumental to the development of this work.
"The Hinge Trees" is a response to Kevin Giese's sculpture, "Immigrant,"
which can be found at Lynden Sculpture Garden.

This book is set in Centaur & Candara
by the Center for Literary Publishing
at Colorado State University.
Copyediting by Brianna Rivers.
Book design & typesetting by Anamika Dugger.
Proofreading by Lincoln Greenhaw.
Cover design by Kaelyn Riley.
Printing by BookMobile.